Snake Chinese Horoscope 2023

By
IChingHun FengShuisu

Table of Contents

Introduce

The character of people born in the year of the SNAKE

People born in this year speak less and have cute faces. Anyone who sees it is likely to be persistent and charming. Loved by others, speaks little, avoids gossip, and has good manners. People this year have never been in debt, and know how to save, but are sluggish. But being a thinker is beneficial. A wise and determined individual who does not abandon anything in the middle of the road. People born in the Year of the Snake trust first impressions, feelings, sympathy, advice, and other people's opinions. incorporating the sixth sense into decision-making.

Even if he is a person who likes to talk less, when he has spoken, he often speaks exaggeratedly. Another is a good lie. No matter how big or small and survive every time. People born this year love to flirt and have sex, but not too nasty. So people come to fall in love with this year's man with a big head, because they are romantic, very jealous, like to have high expectations, want to feel confident, and are always safe.

Strength:
You are a scholar who is intelligent and enjoys learning.
Weaknesses:
You're narcissistic and self-sufficient.

Love:
People born in this year have a lot of boyfriends. Because so much love must confront the chaos of love until it hurts. There is always a love that is so hot and flirtatious that it cannot keep up. Some people may not have a unique partnership with whom to demonstrate their charm. Old women and widows are buzzing, even though they are not attractive or attractive. because your grace's style and eloquence It's so catchy, don't tell anyone Flirting extends to even the smallest snake people. However, if someone is already a fan, I can assure you that I am the most envious. Do not allow anyone to interfere. Most

importantly, I enjoy being selfish and impatient.

Suitable Career:
Because Snakes are fire-elemental, those born in the year of the Snake should pursue a career related to fire, such as opening a shop for electrical or electronic devices such as radios, and televisions, or selling electrical appliances. Open a gas station, or pursue a career that necessitates specific skills, such as being a speaker, critic, judge, prosecutor, teacher, writer, politician, journalist, beautician, photographer, makeup artist, or model. Modeling, selling artificial plants, trees, and flowers, fortune telling in various fields, the military, and law enforcement are all suitable professions for those born in the year of the Snake.

Year of the SNAKE (Gold) | (1941) & (2001)

"The Snake in hibernation" is a person born in the year of the SNAKE at the age of 82 years (1941) and 22 years (2001)

Overview

For the senior destiny, which is around the age of 82 this year, the planet orbiting into your destiny is The "Star God of Destruction," which causes family strife and chaos. However, the most important issue this year is health. Be especially cautious of illnesses. You should also be wary of conflicts between family members' children. Should not intervene or interfere with the children's problems. If you have the opportunity, make time to make merit by praying to monks, listening to sermons, making merit, giving alms, spreading mercy, and redeeming the lives of animals. It will not only make you feel calmer and happier, but it will also make your suffering less severe. Furthermore, you should keep your emotions in check and let go of any issues that arise in your physical and mental health.

The planet that orbits into your destiny this year for a 22-year-old Snake year is "Dao Kuang Soo" (Dow Chains). This year is the year of the ardent people who want to be themselves and seek the way they want. which the search is not incorrect However, you must be able to distinguish between right and wrong because society has both positive and negative aspects. There are both good and bad people in the world. Graduates will lead you to results if you are in a relationship with them. However, if you are in a relationship with the wrong person, you may face a prison sentence. So, if a friend invites you to do something dangerous, decline. You should think about it carefully. Because having fun for a while or attempting to do something bad once can completely change your life. You may meet untrustworthy people and be duped as a result of your fate. As a result, it should be known that refusing some, including travel, should not be taken lightly. Take precautions to avoid mishaps.

Career and Business

The horoscope for the seedling seat predicts the fate of this year's work. Those who are still studying will be able to study both inside and outside the country and have a bright future. Anyone who has entered the labor force can do any job. However, you should do what you enjoy and are good at so that you don't stress and can work happily. To keep up with the ever-changing world, you must also continue to improve yourself. The months in which your work and studies are bright and prosperous are: 12th month of China (5 Jan. - 3 Feb.), 2nd month of China (6 Mar. - 4 Apr), 4th month of China (6 May – 5 Jun) and the 8th month of China (8 Sep. – 7 Oct.), but if entering the 1st month of China (4 Feb. – 5 Mar.), the 5th month of China (6 Jun - 6 Jul) 7th month of China (8 Aug - 7 Sep) and 10th month of China (7 Nov - 6 Dec) You should exercise caution. If there is a contract document, you should carefully consider your obligations before accepting work or requesting funding so that you do not have to sit and worry.

Financial

Throughout the year, the story of the fortunes of the destiny for both this year's age is uncertain. As a result, you should start saving and managing your money as soon as possible. Anything that isn't necessary should be removed. The best way to plan your finances and save money should be maintained. It will not be stuck if any date appears unexpected current expenditure or if there is an emergency. This year, seniors should consider investing in a variety of fields. Even if the profits are good, if it is illegal and immoral, it should be avoided because it jeopardizes your wallet and reputation. In particular, you need to be very careful during the following months: 1st month of China (4 Feb. – 5 Mar.), the 5th month of China (6 Jun – 6 Jul), 7th month of China (8 Aug. – 7 Sep.) and 10th month of China (7 Nov. – 6 Dec.) forbidding others to borrow money and receive guarantees. Should not gamble, gamble, whether on football, horses, boxing, or others because they have the right to lose insolvent and will lead you to problems that do not struggle. Furthermore, do not invest in illegal and immoral businesses because they risk jail time. The months with good financial turnover are the 12th month of China (5 Jan. – 3 Feb.), the 2nd month of China (6 Mar. – 4 Apr), the 4th month of China (6 May – 5 Jun), and the 8th month of China (8 Sep. – 7 Oct.).

Family

Because in the house of destiny appeared, this year's family horoscope lacked peace. "Dao Nguyuki," "Bad Star Noose Sing," and "Dao Kua Hoo" cling to the group to focus on harassment. Which will harm you in a variety of ways, including family squabbles, unexpected accidents, health issues, lawsuits, and criminal penalties. As a result, trusting is not a trivial matter; at the very least, you should be consistent in your carelessness. Take precautions to ensure the safety of your family members. Be careful not to make a mistake, tell a story, or infringe on anyone's rights so that you are not sued. And this year must prioritize home health care for the elderly and young children. The months that you need to be especially careful are: the 1st month of China (4 Feb. – 5 Mar.), 5th month of China (6 Jun. – 6 Jul.), 7th month of China (8 Aug. – 7 Sep), and the 10th month of China (7 Nov – 6 Dec), both in terms of unexpected dangers. Being harassed and cautious will be mourning for the elders during this period.

Love

This year's love falls and waits on the seat. As a result, you cannot rush to do whatever you want, and it is a matter of voluntariness that cannot be resisted. People who have earned the right to reconnect in this life will find it easy to agree. People who have never demonstrated any merit would be difficult to achieve. However, you have plenty of time to find the right person. You will be more disappointed if you are impatient and reckless. Importantly, during the following months, the Lord of Destiny should be careful of chaos and quarrels, including the 1st month of China (4 Feb. – 5 Mar.), the 5th month of China (6 Jun. – 6 Jul.), The 7th month of China (8 Aug. – 7 Sep.) and the 10th month of China (7 Nov. – 6 Dec.), You must be more cautious of fluctuations. Those of you who have a loving partner should be cautious of the third hand that comes in the middle to cause misunderstandings and should avoid going to various entertainment venues that will bring trouble and trouble.

Health

This year has not been kind to your health. Especially during the months that you should add extra to your physical health, such as the 1st month of China (4 Feb. – 5 Mar.), the 5th month of China (6 Jun. – 6 Jul.), the 7th month of China (8 Aug. – 7 Sep.) and 10th month of China (7 Nov. – 6 Dec.) Congenital or chronic diseases, as well as foodborne illness venom, should be avoided by the elderly. Regarding the fate of adolescence, please avoid intoxicants. If you drink, you should not drive a car or operate machinery, and you should be cautious not to be careless.

Year of the SNAKE (Water) | (1953) & (2013)

" The SNAKE in the grass " is a person born in the year of the SNAKE at the age of 70 years (1953) and 10 years (2013)

Overview

Because the planet orbiting into the senior destiny around the age of 70 this year is the "shackle star," its influence will cause you to become entangled in chaos until you can't get out of it. As a result, this year should be characterized by recklessness. Specifically, health issues, arguments, conflicts with others, and the occurrence of stories from subordinates or children that will spread to become a major cause of loss and destruction of peace will be a major cause of loss and destruction of peace. So, this year, avoid becoming involved in other people's problems. Remember that as an adult, you must be fair and neutral, and you must avoid retaliation. Finally, the troublemaker will be defeated and will leave on their own. In addition, be aware of any conflicts or diseases that may arise among household members. You must either mourn an elder or someone close to you. The best way to start the year is to find time to pay respect to the gods and make merit after merit.

For children born in the Year of the Snake, around the age of ten, the planet that orbits into your destiny this year is "Dao Noose Sing" (Star God of Disaster), so parents may have to be more restrictive than usual in terms of education. In terms of activities and going out to play this year. Parents should not overlook safety and should advise their children to exercise caution when participating in various activities. Bring a revered sacred relic with you if you have to travel long distances to camp, camp, or go out for activities in the countryside. When traveling by land or sea, be aware of potential hazards. Parents should look for an opportunity to take their children to pay their respects to God for relief at the start of the year.

Career and Business

This year, the direction of destiny's trade fluctuates up and down. The best way to find a successor is to help relieve the hard work. Also, in business, you should have two or three plans in place to support or initiate a small project this year. When you are successful, you punch and expand to achieve the goal without error. And they should plan ahead of time in terms of funding, manpower, and management methods. If you want to invest in your career and see it as a chance, The appropriate time should be acted upon immediately. There will be a lovely return. Especially the months in which work and trade are booming, such as the 12th month of China (5 Jan. – 3 Feb.), the 2nd month of China (6 Mar. – 4 Apr.), the 4th month of China (6 May – 5 Jun) and the 8th month of China (8 Sep. – 7 Oct.), but if entering the 1st month of China (4 Feb. – 5 Mar.), the 5th month of China (6 Jun – 6 Jul), China (8 Aug. – 7 Sep.) and month of China (7 Nov. – 6 Dec.) You should be prepared to deal with interpersonal conflicts and contract documents. The nuances should be given careful consideration.

Financial

The financial outlook for this year is bleak, and working capital will be insufficiently liquid. Don't be so preoccupied with small profits that you stock up on unprofitable items. Because sometimes the additional items are slow to sell, causing the capital to sink in with the goods. Even if the discount increases, if it disrupts working capital and continues to pay interest, the outcome is not secure. The best way to avoid financial trouble this year is to save money and carefully plan your finances. During the month that your finances will stumble, such as the 1st month of China (4 Feb. – 5 Mar.), the 5th month of China (6 Jun – 6 Jul.), the 7th month of China (8 Aug. – 7 Sep.) and 10th month of China (7 Nov – 6 Dec), who should not be allowed to lend money and receive guarantees. Gambling and investing in illegal businesses should also be avoided, as should not know how to cut costs and unprofitable parts. For the months with the good financial flow, namely, the 12th month of China (5 Jan. – 3 Feb.), the 2nd month of China (6 Mar. – 4 Apr.), the 4th month of China (6 May – 5 Jun) and the 8th month of China (8 Sep. – 7 Oct.).

Family

This year's family luck has been rough. Children of this age should be wary of the power of conflict in their homes. This year, the house should be organized to bring the members of the house together. To be respectful and respectful, one must not believe in one's superiority. Do not dismiss the wisdom of an elder. The elders, on the other hand, must know how to behave properly. Do not meddle in the affairs of children and do not use emotions to solve problems. A good role model is required. Children will be thoughtful. Months that will cause chaos in the house include the 1st month of China (4 Feb. – 5 Mar.), the 5th month of China (6 Jun – 6 Jul), 7th month of China (8 Aug. – 7 Sep.), and the 10th month of China (7 Nov. – 6 Dec.) That the fate of both ages should increase caution in all aspects, including accidents and quarrels, as well as beware of lost or stolen valuables.

Love

The love horoscope is nothing special. This year, however, you have the opportunity to make merit with your lover or spouse or to participate in a long-distance trip to strengthen your love. But should be careful during the months when love is prone to conflicts, such as the 1st month of China (4 Feb. – 5 Mar.), the 5th month of China (6 Jun. – 6 Jul.), the 7th month of China (8 Aug. – 7 Sep.) and 10th month of China (7 Nov. – 6 Dec.) where you should behave appropriately and serve as a role model for the younger generation you must avoid wandering around at nightlife and orbits for your children to be respected. Because there may be issues that cause you to lose your respectability, and avoid interfering in other people's families. Avoid causing squabbles with insiders and causing disruptions in the house.

Health

The fate is not in good health this year. You were required to spend a long time in and out of the hospital because your health would deteriorate due to the influence of the evil stars. As a result, you should take special care of your health, keeping an eye out for problems with blood pressure, brain diseases, heart disease, embolism, food poisoning, and fainting, which can lead to accidents in unsupported months. If you go anywhere, have a follower to take care of closely. For children's health, be careful using sharp tools that can cause injury. And be careful of accidents, especially during the following months: 1st month of China (4 Feb. – 5 Mar.), 5th month of China (6 Jun – 6 Jul), 7th month of China (8 Aug. – 7 Sep), and the 10th month of China (7 Nov. – 6 Dec.).

Year of the SNAKE (Wood) | (1965)

" The snake of merit" is a person born in the year of the SNAKE at the age of 58 years (1965)

Overview

This year is a disaster year because the planet orbiting your destiny house is "The Deity of Disaster," and this star is a planet of disaster. When fate rules, it often causes frustration and resentment, and it also brings problems and illnesses, in addition to having to keep solving fussy problems. This year, your behavior should be humble rather than boastful or insulting to others. When it comes to being with children, you should focus on kindness and avoid interfering in matters that are not your concern. Despite the presence of a dangerous planet, "The God of Destiny" is in the house of destiny. However, an auspicious star named "Sukwasana" is orbiting to assist. This will help to lighten the burden. On the commercial side, you'll find sponsors assisting many things to go through for business expansion. You can achieve excellent results by investing at the end of the year. Concerning the family, there is something to be aware of: the health problems of the people in the house, particularly the elderly and children. During the year, you must mourn an adult relative. They should also be wary of the chaos that will descend on the family. Conflicts and quarrels are the root causes of unrest. To avoid obstacles, any action must always be conscious.

Career and Business

This will help to lighten the burden. On the commercial side, you'll find sponsors assisting many things to go through for business expansion. You can achieve excellent results by investing at the end of the year. Concerning the family, there is something to be aware of: the health problems of the people in the house, particularly the elderly and children. During the year, you must mourn an adult relative.

They should also be wary of the chaos that will descend on the family. Conflicts and quarrels are the root causes of unrest. To avoid obstacles, any action must always be conscious. Especially the months in which work flourishes, such as the 12th month of China (5 Jan. – 3 Feb.), the 2nd month of China (6 Mar. – 4 Apr.), the 4th month of China (6 May. – 5 Jun.) and the 8th month of China (8 Sep. – 7 Oct.), but if entering the 1st month of China (4 Feb. – 5 Mar.), the 5th month of China (6 Jun. – 6 Jul.) 7th month of China (8 Aug. – 7 Sep.) and 10th month of China (7 Nov. – 6 Dec.). You must exercise extreme caution. Be careful not to disadvantage the parties when contracting for or accepting employment. As a result, before signing any contract documents, the documents should be carefully reviewed.

Financial

The financial outlook for this year is moderate; direct cash flows from sales of goods, services, or salary income will continue to flow in and are healthy. However, the extra money or money from gambling is uncertain if extremely greedy people have the right to be hurt. You should avoid being punished if your business is insulting to illegal or immoral acts. Especially during the month when the financial star is down and you have to manage your money carefully, such as the 1st month of China (4 Feb. – 5 Mar.), the 5th month of China (6 Jun. – 6 Jul.), the 7th month of China (8 Aug. – 7 Sep.) and 10th month of China (7 Nov. – 6 Dec.) Prohibit accepting financial guarantees for others. And beware of the twist of luck that may cause insomnia. The months that your finances will have better liquidity are the 12th month of China (5 Jan. – 3 Feb.), the 2nd month of China (6 Mar. – 4 Apr.), the 4th month of China (6 May – 5 Jun), and the 8th month of China (8 Sep. – 7 Oct.).

Family

Because of the influence of the evil star this year, the family horoscope is not favorable. You must monitor the health of the elderly in the house, who may become seriously ill to the point of mourning for elderly relatives, and keep an eye out for unforeseen events such as accidents. It will happen to the household members. Especially during the months when the family will have trouble, such as the 1st month of China (4 Feb. – 5 Mar.), the 5th month of China (6 Jun. – 6 Jul.), the 7th month of China (8 Aug - 7 Sept.) and 10th month of China (7 Nov. - 6 Dec.) Be wary of elder harassment or suffering at the hands of servants or domestic servants. Be wary of valuables in the house that have been lost or stolen, as well as accidents caused by the use of various devices in the house.

Love

The love horoscope for this year is mediocre. Even though there is some commotion about each other. However, if you don't take it too seriously, it will benefit your marriage. But destiny had to be cautious with his words. Because what you say can have an impact, even if it is unintentional. However, it has an impact on the other party's feelings. As a result, I implore you to give careful consideration to our hearts, tongues, and teeth for us to coexist in peace. The months that often have quarrels and disagreements are 1st month of China (4 Feb. – 5 Mar.), 5th month of China (6 Jun. – 6 Jul.), the 7th month of China (8 Aug. - 7 Sep.), and the

10th month of China (7 Nov. - 6 Dec.), where it is forbidden to become involved in other people's family matters and where it is important to listen to other people's problems You should be aware and firm with each other. At the same time, avoid going to entertainment venues and do not listen to or pay attention to malicious gossip.

Health

Your health is not good this year. You should be aware that insomnia or insomnia is a precursor to other diseases. The most common cause is stress. Problems that can't be solved, worries, and overthinking about yourself If you are feeling unwell, the best thing to do is to consult a doctor. Another thing to keep in mind is drinking and eating hygiene. Tobacco use should be limited. Especially during the months that you need to pay special attention to health care, such as the 1st month of China (4 Feb. – 5 Mar.), the 5th month of China (6 Jun. – 6 Jul.), the 7th month of China (8 Aug - 7 Sept.) and the 10th month of China (7 Nov. 6 Dec.) During climate change, we must be cautious of air allergies and epidemics. Because it can spread to other diseases, be cautious after consuming intoxicating beverages that could cause an accident.

Year of the SNAKE (Fire) | (1977)

" The SNAKE evolves from the cave" is a person born in the year of the SNAKE at the age of 46 years (1977)

Overview

Even though the planet that orbits into your destiny this year is the "shackle star," it is another auspicious year for your life cycle because it has been supported by many shining auspicious stars. As a result, those who assist those in government service or work in various agencies will have a better chance of advancement. For those who do business, although the trade appears to be quite hectic, the rewards will be well worth the effort. It's known as working hard to amass a large amount of wealth. So don't be disheartened because the future looks promising. This year, good relationship skills with both supervisors and subordinates should be developed and maintained, as should the use of morality in personnel management. Because collaboration will double people's progress in every work activity this year. However, because there is a star aimed at it in the house of destiny. You will need a lot of patience and diligence this year. You should think carefully before acting. Because your destiny this year will face a stumbling block that could lead to failure. Be cautious, the elders will cause harm. Furthermore, you should be aware of any accidents that may occur during the journey. Both should take care of their health as well as the health of their family members regularly.

Career and Business

The fate of this year's work is dependent on the ability to sit. As a result, we must go through numerous trials to solve various problems. Communication and interpersonal skills must be improved this year. Meet regularly with people who need to contact both customers and partners. Must be able to strengthen relationships and generate goodwill with sincerity. Understand how to pay attention and look after colleagues and subordinates. Encourage him to pay attention to us. If you can accomplish this, it will significantly reduce the operation's barriers and conflicts. Especially during the month when work will encounter obstacles, problems include 1st month of China (4 Feb. – 5 Mar.), 5th month of China (6 Jun. – 6 Jul.), 7th month of China (8 Aug. – 7 Sep), and 10th month of China (7 Nov. – 6 Dec.), where your work is quite difficult Employment contracts or employment contracts must be carefully drafted. Be wary of hidden obligations that will disadvantage you. The months in which work and trade are smooth and bright are: 12th month of China (5 Jan. - 3 Feb.), 2nd month of China (6 Mar. - 4 Apr), 4th month of China (6 May. – 5 Jun.) and the 8th month of China (8 Sep. – 7 Oct.).

Financial

Even though the financial and fortune criteria are moderate, there are periods of uncertainty with a high potential for reversals. There will be unanticipated expenses that cause you to lose liquidity. As a result, financial planning should be done throughout the year. Having money set aside, including savings, eliminates unnecessary expenses. Finding a way to supplement your income will allow you to live comfortably during the financial crisis. You should be especially careful during the following months: 1st month of China (4 Feb. – 5 Mar.), 5th month of China (6 Jun. – 6 Jul.), 7th month of China (8 Aug. – 7 Sep.), and 10th month of China (7 Nov. – 6 Dec.) who should not be allowed to lend money and receive guarantees Do not be avaricious. Extremely greedy for the property of others, which will only exacerbate the problem. Furthermore, should not invest or conduct business that is contrary to the law and morality. The months with the good financial flow are the 12th month of China (5 Jan. – 3 Feb.), the 2nd month of China (6 Mar. – 4 Apr), the 4th month of China (6 May. – 5 Jun), and the 8th month of China (8 Sep. – 7 Oct.).

Family

This year's family horoscope has both positive and negative aspects. You should be concerned about the safety of your family members. Keep an eye out for children or servants who are causing trouble or causing damage. Your valuables are safe when you are not at home. It should be carefully stored, and people in the salt should be cautious of war warms entering the house. Electrical appliances, wires, and tools that are damaged should be properly repaired to avoid accidents. Because during the 1st month of China (4 Feb. – 5 Mar.), the 5th month of China (6 Jun. – 6 Jul.), the 7th month of China (8 Aug. – 7 Sep.) and the 10th month of China (7 Nov – 6 Dec), When the fate of the family is at stake, be wary of sickness and sickness in the home. Accidents caused by the use of tools or equipment failure should be avoided. Be wary of employees using the wrong tools, which can lead to unexpected incidents and damage, and if any incidents occur, you must be aware of them and listen to them before passing judgment on others. Because it could be fuel, resulting in disaster later.

Love

This year's love horoscope is not favorable. You and your loved ones are prone to squabbles and fights. Both fate and destiny must be wary of nonsense behavior. The desire to wander will destroy the sweetness and deprive the home of peace. Especially during the months when the love of destiny is fragile and easy to argue, such as the 1st month of China (4 Feb. – 5 Mar.), the 5th month of China (6 Jun – 6 Jul.)) the 7th month of China (8 Aug. – 7 Sep.) and the 10th month of China (7 Nov. – 6 Dec.) You will have to be firm. Listen to no gossip, slander, or slander. You should also not meddle in other people's family matters. Avoid going to places of entertainment, including the source of malice. Also, keep in mind that a third hand may come between you two during this time.

Health

This year's health is not looking good. At the start of the year, you should avoid not getting enough sleep and eating unsanitary food, which can lead to food poisoning. Be wary of migraine headaches, which can cause problems. Furthermore, diabetes and other congenital diseases are expected to worsen this year. This year, however, you should prioritize regular check-ups, as well as work, family, and rest time. Don't overwork or stress yourself. The months you need to be very careful about your health are 1st month of China (4 Feb. 5 Mar.), 5th month of China (6 Jun. - 6 Feb.), 7th month of China (8 Aug. – 7 Sep.), and the 10th month of China (7 Nov. – 6 Dec.) where you must be extra cautious to avoid injury. And, if you drink alcohol or have a hangover, do not drive or operate machinery because it may result in an accident, and be cautious when operating road vehicles.

Year of the SNAKE (Earth) | (1989)

" The Snake In the river" is a person born in the year of the SNAKE at the age of 34 years (1989)

Overview

Because the planet influencing your fate this year is As a result, his life this year demanded a great deal of patience and adaptability. Please keep in mind that life is a struggle. Those who can stand their ground in the face of difficulties and obstacles are capable of outperforming others. Resist the winds and storms when the winds are calm, the skies are clear, and the road ahead is smoother than it was yesterday. As a result, fate will find a bad star aiming in the stars even this year, but if you are determined consciously and live recklessly, you will be able to deal with all kinds of problems without difficulty. However, you should be cautious of your health and the elderly in the house, as well as of safety and accidents while working and traveling. Furthermore, there may be a friend this year who does not wish to lead you in an orbit and persuade you to leave the road. May you be careful not to become intoxicated in the presence of well-wishers, so that your loss is minimized.

Career and Business

They work for those who work full-time or for the government. Those who start this year will have the opportunity to change jobs or be promoted. But it takes perseverance and patience. The ability to adapt and constantly add knowledge to yourself for the results to be visible. For those considering coming out to start their own business. This year is favorable for establishing yourself as a business owner. However, you must expend twice as much perseverance. To have the opportunity, they must also know how to adjust their skills in good human relations with those around them. The month that promotes his work and trade is prosperous, such as the 12th month of China (5 Jan. - 3 Feb.), the 2nd month of China (6 Mar. - 4 Apr.), the 4th month of China (6 May – 5 Jun) and the 8th month of China (8 Sep. – 7 Oct.), but if entering the 1st month of China (4 Feb. – 5 Mar.) 5 China (6 Jun – 6 Jul) 7th month of China (8 Aug. – 7 Sep.) and 10th month of China (7 Nov. – 6 Dec.) This year's work and investment must be cautious and may be deceiving. Furthermore, the employment contract or employment should not be rushed and should be carefully considered. Otherwise, it may turn into a contract that will harm you in the future.

Financial

Even though this year's financial horoscope includes monsoons, The first six months will be exciting, but at a manageable level. If you are prepared and have a good plan in place from the start, make sure to carefully plan your spending and look for ways to increase your income. Finances will be more stable in the next six months. Because cash inflows are plentiful, both from salaries and from fortune. And if persistence persists, does not compromise on hardships, during the 12th month of China (5 Jan. - 3 Feb.), the 2nd month of China (6 Mar. - 4 Apr), the 4th month of China (6 May. - 5 Jun.) and the 8th month of China (8 Sep - 7 Oct), you will have a good income as you wish. However, if entering the 1st month of China (4 Feb. – 5 Mar.), the 5th month of China (6 Jun. – 6 Jul.), 7th month of China (8 Aug. – 7 Jul.), and the 10th month of China (7 Nov. – 6 Dec.), You will run into liquidity issues. As a result, speculative investments with varying degrees of risk should be avoided. And should not lend money to anyone. Including not putting on a brave face to accept guarantees to assist anyone.

Family

This year's family will be somewhat uneasy because there will be stories about minors or servants in the house causing conflicts and arguments that will disrupt the peace of the family members. They must also be mindful of health issues in the home, including both the elderly and children. Both of you meet the criteria for mourning your elderly relatives. Things will frequently cause you anxiety, especially in the first six months. However, everything will return to normal in the next six months. There will be peace, and there may be an auspicious or joyful event in the house. This year is mild for relatives and friends. But be cautious when dating your friends and don't completely believe them. By the month that you need to be careful about family and friends, and relatives, such as the 1st month of China (4 Feb. – 5 Mar.), the 5th month of China (6 Jun. – 6 Jul.), the 7th month of China (8 Aug. – 7 Sep.) and 10th month of China (7 Nov. – 6 Dec.) During these times, you should do your job well. Avoid interfering with family and friends or getting involved in other people's conflicts. And it's also a good time to learn to say no to friends who want to invite you to parties.

Love

The love horoscope for this year is considered normal and happy. Even if you disagree with each other, be patient and talk rationally. You should talk about facing each other or letting them pass a little rather than revving the seams. Because it only magnifies small things, and you should be careful with your own words. Indifference includes a lack of empathy for a partner or partners. It will spark debate. Especially during the months when love is quite fragile, such as the 1st month of China (4 Feb. – 5 Mar.), the 5th month of China (6 Jun. – 6 Jul.), the 7th month of China (8 Aug. - 7 Sep) and the 10th month of China (7 Nov. - 6 Dec.), be careful of third parties to intervene to cause misunderstandings to spread into a big story.

Health

During the first six months of the year, you should be on the lookout for allergies, colds, and headaches. As a result, you should get enough rest. Make time for sports or exercise. This will help to alleviate these symptoms. Your health will improve over the next six months. If you have a congenital disease, you will see a good doctor or receive the appropriate medication to treat it. But still need to increase caution if entering the 1st month of China (4 Feb. – 5 Mar.), the 5th month of China (6 Jun. – 6 Jul.), 7th month of China (8 Aug. – 7 Sep.), and the 10th month of China (7 Nov – 6 Dec) that may have accidents from work, travel. Being careful with the use of tools will cause disaster to the point of bleeding rubber out.

Chinese Astrology Horoscope for Each Month

Month 12 in the Tiger Year (6 Jan 23 - 3 Feb 23)
This month's horoscope has received good energy from many orbiting auspicious stars that shine in support, thus helping to brighten the direction of the fortune's finances and work in this month. Many components fit better. As a result, the most important thing you should do during this time is prioritized tasks and problems. They should be resolved as soon as possible so that they do not accumulate and cause old problems to reoccur.

During this time, you will discover new ways or channels to overcome old obstacles in your field of work, and it is considered a good time to increase your work, make sales, or expand production and trade. However, the details must still be thoroughly examined. Remember to be patient in everything you do. Don't let your emotions control you. Most importantly, you must carry out your responsibilities to the best of your ability. Do not interfere with the work of others.

This salary horoscope is adequate. You also have salary income and sales available. However, the money of fortune floats around gambling. It's better not to risk it than to get hurt.

This month's family horoscope will bring you good news about your child's work or education at home. A happy family is full of smiles and reconciliation.

Health should be taken into consideration; not getting enough rest will result in latent disease in the future.

For those who are waiting for responses from the other party, the love horoscope is smooth. You will receive results that are precise as expected.

Support Days: 3 Jan., 7 Jan., 11 Jan., 15 Jan., 19 Jan., 23 Jan., 27 Jan., 31 Jan.
Lucky Days: 2 Jan., 14 Jan., 26 Jan.
Misfortune Days: 5 Jan., 17 Jan., 29 Jan.
Bad Days: 8 Jan., 20 Jan.

Month 1 in the Rabbit Year (4 Feb 23 - 5 Mar 23)
This month, although the situation around me appears to be volatile and uncertain. However, establishing a foothold and utilizing intelligence to help determine the plan will aid in tightening the issue of uncertainty. and observe the clear results for some progress

During this period, commercial work encountered obstacles and was halted. You must exercise extreme caution. First, see clearly and prepare thoroughly. Take action now. Furthermore, you should use your skills to establish positive relationships with those you need to contact, whether they are your boss or not. Servants, as well as those with whom they do business and customers must have the humility to help you overcome the obstacles.

A component of the joint venture It is not appropriate to put it off.

This salary horoscope is not favorable. low income, high spending As a result, it should be cost-effective and look for ways to generate additional income through other channels. Do not take chances with your luck. Do not be avaricious. Because there are criteria that can be manipulated.

Families who are not at peace should be cautious of illness and accidents in the home.

For love is ordinary. However, you should avoid going to entertainment venues to reduce other problems that may arise.

Health should be cautious of latent diseases that may attack or old congenital diseases that may recur.

When traveling, be cautious of accidents.

Support Days: 4 Feb., 8 Feb., 12 Feb., 16 Feb., 20 Feb., 24 Feb., 28 Feb.
Lucky Days: 7 Feb., 19 Feb.
Misfortune Days: 10 Feb., 22 Feb.
Bad Days: 1 Feb., 13 Feb., 25 Feb.

Month 2 in the Rabbit Year (6 Mar 23 - 5 Apr 23)
This month's journey has been smoother than the previous month's. Job responsibilities, including the fateful trading business, are also supported by adults and those around them, assisting in turning the crisis into an opportunity. As a result, the work finds a path of progress and prosperity as an opportunity to expand both the results and the sales to shine once more.

On this occasion, you should look for low-risk investment opportunities and understand how to generate sales from an expanding market. Constantly expanding your knowledge and understanding of how to plan your management for the entire year will undoubtedly yield abundant rewards for you.

This salary horoscope is favorable. Sales of goods and services generate two-way cash inflows. Furthermore, commissions, dividends, and money from fortune are added to the pocket. This is the month when your finances are in good shape.

The family horoscope found auspicious energy to visit the house at this time, allowing the planning of auspicious events. Whether it's relocating to a new home, relocating to a new workplace, establishing a new branch, or adding new members.

The love story is the season when fragrant and sweet love flowers bloom. There will be joy during this time. Say a bird pointed at the wood and said the wood followed

Health is better, but you must maintain it regularly.

During this time, relatives and friends are extremely helpful.

Support Days: 4 Mar, 8 Mar., 12 Mar., 16 Mar., 20 Mar., 24 Mar., 28 Mar.
Lucky Days: 3 Mar, 15 Mar., 27 Mar.
Misfortune Days: 6 Mar, 18 Mar., 30 Mar.
Bad Days: 9 Mar, 21 Mar.

Month 3 in the Rabbit Year (6 Apr 23 - 5 May 23)
This month, your destiny has collided with the month in which Chong Clash has caused the road of life to deteriorate. Obstacles and unevenness gradually accumulated and formed, resulting in an eruption. It will have a significant impact on finances and investments, in particular.

The following are the main things you should do this month: Several backup plans must be prepared to deal with and solve problems that will arise in a variety of forms. Which necessitates dedicated efforts to overcome obstacles even when regular cash flows in continuously. However, extra money falls into the star of loss, so do not gamble, gamble, or accept guarantees on behalf of others, and avoid being overly greedy and investing in risky businesses. There are numerous obstacles in this period of trade work. However, if a problem arises, please do not use your emotions or impatience to solve it; it will be easier to resolve.

This month, families are also concerned about the health of their elderly and children at home. Both fates have criteria for attending the prayer ceremony. Both should be wary of the little or servant who is causing trouble.

In terms of love, the opposite sex will assist you this month. So, there's nothing to be concerned about. However, health is still an issue. Be wary of mishaps and food poisoning.

Support Days: 1 Apr., 5 Apr., 9 Apr., 13 Apr., 17 Apr., 21 Apr., 25 Apr., 29 Apr.
Lucky Days: 8 Apr., 20 Apr.
Misfortune Days: 11 Apr., 23 Apr.
Bad Days: 2 Apr., 14 Apr., 26 Apr.

Month 4 in the Rabbit Year (6 May 23 - 5 Jun 23)
Your destiny graph, which was born this month, is heading in the right direction. Because many auspicious stars are still standing and not moving, the fuss and chaos in the last month have been minimal.

The routine work is going well. However, you should not be complacent and should seize this opportunity by creating additional work or expanding new work channels. If you are brave and diligent, go to work, seize every opportunity that comes your way, and wait for the right moment. You will see significant results that are well worth the effort. Whatever seed is planted will bear fruit. You will get a lot of returns if you add more diligence.

This salary horoscope is favorable; there will be unexpected income. However, you should plan to allocate various investments wisely, particularly gambling. Gambling or investing in illegal and immoral businesses should be avoided because it will stifle liquidity and cause you to suffer.

This month's family is content. However, some tasks should not be delegated to children. Because the work will be harmed, you must select the right person for the job and may require additional care.

For love, be cautious of unfaithful thinking or going to a service location that may be infected with the disease and thus dangerous.

Be cautious of various infectious diseases that may occur in the gastrointestinal tract, according to your horoscope. You must maintain proper hygiene. They continue to support one another as relatives and friends.

Support Days: 3 May., 7 May., 11 May., 15 May., 19 May., 23 May., 27 May., and 31 May.
Lucky Days: 2 May., 14 May., and 26 May.
Misfortune Days: 5 May., 17 May., 29 May.
Bad Days: 8 May., 20 May.

Month 5 in the Rabbit Year (6 Jun 23 - 6 Jul 23)
This month's destiny is referred to as having to support yourself. Even though the threshold of

destiny has not dropped significantly, obstacles and unevenness remain. This month, you should work quickly to complete any outstanding tasks. Take the problem as a learning experience and devise a solution to prevent it from happening again. Find the root cause gradually and solve each problem one at a time. You should let go of any problem that is beyond your control. Don't be too concerned. Simply request that you do your best based on the factors and strengths that you have.

The direction of trade work has improved slightly this month. There will be a change in the job, which may result in a change in the job or responsibilities. However, external investments in various areas should be avoided during this period.

This salary, direct income continues to flow smoothly, but you should not be undervalued. The best approach should be to carefully guard accounting documents. To identify weaknesses to prevent financial leaks and to identify strengths, new channels will bring 2-3 additional income streams. Money earned from gambling or stock lottery speculation should be invested wisely.

The family horoscope for this month is calm. However, it appears that conflicts in love are easy to argue about. Be wary of a minor disagreement that can quickly escalate into a major issue. As a result, you must remain calm and maintain good emotional control. In terms of health, keep an eye out for air allergies, colds, and injuries to the legs or knees.

This month is auspicious for relatives and friends to travel to make merit or to assist in public charity work together.

Support Days: 4 Jun., 8 Jun., 12 Jun., 16 Jun., 20 Jun., 24 Jun., 28 Jun.
Lucky Days: 7 Jun., 19 Jun.
Misfortune Days: 10 Jun., 22 Jun.
Bad Days: 1 Jun., 13 Jun., 25 Jun.

Month 6 in the Rabbit Year (7 Jul 23 - 7 Aug 23)

Because of your discouragement, your destiny born in the year of the Snake this month will face one part good and two parts bad. As a result, the work was immersed for an extended period, causing it to be incomplete. This month, here's what you should do. Believe in your point of view and thoughts. Don't listen to what other people say if you think you're doing the right thing and aren't causing trouble for anyone.

In terms of commercial work, you should be aware of management conflicts. Be careful not to be aggressive or hurt others when speaking. If a job change is required during this time, it should be requested to make the work flow more smoothly. Doing activities should be done gradually and not hurriedly because you may fall into a trap that causes even more problems and obstacles than before. Defamation It is preferable to use your actions as evidence than to be offended.

Horoscopes, this salary falls on the seat, wealth loss, and excessive spending. However, fixed income tends to decline. As a result, you should avoid gambling. Don't let anyone borrow money, and keep an eye on your liquidity.

In terms of joining the joint venture, caution is still advised.

The family is still happy. However, the love story is quite feudal. Because of your fluctuating mood, whether good or bad

Minor illnesses such as headaches, stomachaches, or seasonal epidemics will affect health during this time.

Support Days: 2 Jul., 6 Jul., 10 Jul., 14 Jul., 18 Jul., 22 Jul., 26 Jul., 30 Jul.
Lucky Days: 1 Jul., 13 Jul., 25 Jul.
Misfortune Days: 4 Jul., 16 Jul., 28 Jul.
Bad Days: 7 Jul., 19 Jul., 31 Jul.

Month 7 in the Rabbit Year (8 Aug 23 - 7 Sep 23)
This month, your destiny criterion enters the monsoon. Interpersonal conflicts have reappeared as a problem. Work and business will evolve and face challenges. You have the right to enter the battlefield of defeat if you manage it poorly. On this occasion, you should investigate your errors. Identify management flaws

This salary horoscope is not favorable. Keep an eye out for capital outflows. Do not gamble, gamble, or conduct any illegal business. This will only aggravate the financial crisis and drain more funds from it. Starting a new job, and investing in various fields, and starting a new job It's not good, so you should take a break first.

You may need to keep some distance from friends and relatives to help reduce the problem.

The family is wary of conflicts, wary of quarrels, and quarrels among family members until there is no peace. If you are worried or stressed during this time, go to the temple to pay homage to monks, make merit, and meditate. It will aid in having more energy. You should also check in with family members regularly to see if there is a problem and avoid becoming so preoccupied with work that you neglect family members.

You will receive assistance from the opposite sex during this better love month. However, your health is not in good shape. Be wary of shoulder problems, intestinal diseases, and swelling in the body. Be cautious of food and accidents while traveling.

Support Days: 3 Aug., 7 Aug., 11 Aug., 15 Aug., 19 Aug., 23 Aug., 27 Aug., 31 Aug.
Lucky Days: 6 Aug., 18 Aug., 30 Aug.
Misfortune Days: 9 Aug., 21 Aug.
Bad Days: 12 Aug., 24 Aug.

Month 8 in the Rabbit Year (8 Sep 23 - 7 Oct 23)
This month's destiny criterion is that many auspicious stars shine brightly. As a result, work duties and trade activities can run smoothly and efficiently, allowing them to return to their goal. Finances will be in good shape due to high liquidity.

The most important thing you should do during this period is to be diligent in building your work and making more sales to compensate for the previous period. Which does not indicate progress because auspicious stars already exist. In this glorious month, your diligence combined with your destiny will lead you to good career opportunities. They will also meet with customers, solve problems, and take advantage of the opportunity to benefit themselves.

This is an excellent time for a joint venture and other investments.

In this payroll horoscope, cash inflows will come in a variety of forms, allowing you to reap the benefits of your previous investments. And the extra money from the fortune is also eligible to win money; however, beware of greed; even if you are lucky, you can become insolvent.

Find auspicious power for this month's family. House members will be required to purchase expensive assets and will have a higher migration threshold.

The love life is often clattering like tongue and teeth at this time, but if you let it down. It won't be too difficult.

During this time, the body's health is at its peak. You will be strengthened by good news from your family.

Relatives and friends, on the other hand, are in good health. Any problem will be resolved.

Support Days: 4 Sep, 8 Sep., 12 Sep, 16 Sep, 20 Sep., 24 Sep., 28 Sep.
Lucky Days: 11 Sep, 23 Sep.

Misfortune Days: 2 Sep, 14 Sep., 26 Sep.
Bad Days: 5 Sep, 17 Sep., 29 Sep.

Month 9 in the Rabbit Year (8 Oct 23 - 6 Nov 23)

This month's journey has taken a turn for the worse. There will be a collision force, which will result in obstacles. As a result, you must thoroughly examine your business. Because you cannot deny responsibility if an error occurs. Importantly, if every activity is a success, please do not be disappointed because it may later be mocked by others. However, don't be so arrogant that you end up distracting others. Humility will assist you in overcoming adversity.

You will find many jealous people because of your work this month, even if you successfully fall off your seat. To be safe, work with gold on the back of the Buddha statue. You should also take your relationships with those around you seriously and always think before you speak.

During this time, the financial horoscope predicts normal income inflows. However, outside investments or large sums of money should be delayed first. Should not gamble or be overly greedy.

The family is welcoming. There is a helping hand available at this time. However, on the side of love, there will be a rival to compete for love. Both must exercise caution when it comes to passion and devotion. As a result, you must trust and be cautious that disagreements will lead to arguments that will cause cracks in your love life.

For their good, but in the case of relatives and friends, they will find friends who would like to invite them to travel to orbit. As a result, you should avoid and exercise caution.

This opportunity is not suitable for starting a new job or making investments.

Support Days: 2 Oct., 6 Oct., 10 Oct., 14 Oct., 18 Oct., 22 Oct., 26 Oct., 30 Oct.
Lucky Days: 5 Oct., 17 Oct., 29 Oct.
Misfortune Days: 8 Oct., 20 Oct.
Bad Days: 11 Oct., 23 Oct.

Month 10 in the Rabbit Year (7 Nov 23 - 6 Dec 23)

This month, your destiny has returned to meet the power once more, and many evil stars are focusing on disrupting the house of various unstable destinies. Both your work and your finances will be flooded as you prepare to enter the field of editing. Every activity is crammed and uneven. The seat in the field of work was challenged. Be wary of management line conflicts and old problems that keep reappearing to be solved indefinitely. As a result, if you encounter any difficulties during this period, please be patient and do not become discouraged.

The family will have fussy problems and will lack peace due to the little ones or servants causing trouble, and elder relatives may be required to do mourning work. If an auspicious event occurs this month, it will help to dispel the unlucky power.

This salary horoscope was crushed by a broken seat. Something insignificant will cause you to lose a significant amount of wealth. As a result, gambling is prohibited. Do not engage in any illegal business. And you should be cautious about the current expenditure on people in the house, as this will cause you to lose money. It should not be used to spend money on hand during this time. However, gold reserves should always be kept in reserve. Various investments should be avoided during this period.

On the love side of things, it's in a sweet phase; it's not flashy, but it's enough to encourage you to keep fighting.

In poor health, you must be cautious of illnesses and accidents that may cause injury.

In terms of relatives and friends, It's best to avoid dating if you meet a friend who wants to invite you out.

Support Days: 3 Nov., 7 Nov., 11 Nov., 15 Nov., 19 Nov., 23 Nov., 27 Nov.
Lucky Days: 10 Nov., 22 Nov.
Misfortune Days: 1 Nov., 13 Nov., 25 Nov.
Bad Days: 4 Nov., 16 Nov., 28 Nov.

Month 11 in the Rabbit Year (7 Dec 23 - 5 Jan 24)
Regardless of the impact to fall, your destiny criteria this month. However, there are auspicious stars that shine brightly to support and orbit together in the house of destiny, helping to lighten the burden. However, if high-risk work and investment are not experimented with, the chances of failure remain high. As a result, this month is ideal for generating sales results or expanding trade investments in various fields that will yield good returns.

This salary horoscope also provides a useful numerical response. It is sufficient to include money received from gambling, speculation, and floating fortune. But be careful, because you could lose even more. It is preferable to avoid it because it will not protect you. Your financial fortunes this month will be determined by your job horoscope. Do more, get more; do less, get less. As a result, strike the iron while the fire is hot.

This month, there will be a lack of peace within the family, and accidents in the home will put you in danger of being injured, bleeding, or rubber out. As a result, you must regularly inspect electrical appliances, including tools, to ensure that they are in good working order, are not damaged, and are ready for use, and you must be wary of illnesses that may affect other members of the household.

This month's love horoscope is clouded by uncertainty. Those who have a partner must be cautious with third parties and avoid going to various entertainment orbits. There will be some illnesses, but they will be minor. Be cautious of accidents on the road. Let us first leave the issue of cooperation and investment.

Support Days: 1 Dec., 5 Dec., 9 Dec., 13 Dec., 17 Dec., 21 Dec., 25 Dec, 29 Dec.
Lucky Days: 4 Dec., 16 Dec., 28 Dec.
Misfortune Days: 7 Dec., 19 Dec., 31 Dec.
Bad Days: 10 Dec., 22 Dec.

Amulet for The Year of the Snake
"Manjusri Samantabhadra Buddha Ride Elephant"

Those born in the Snake year this year should establish and worship sacred objects. "Manjusri Samantabhadra Buddha Ride Elephant" to increase your luck. By placing it on your desk or cash register, you are requesting mercy. Assist in promoting the smooth growth of destiny's business and trade. wealthy and contented family

(Take note of the orientation in which sacred objects should be established.) It is visible at the end of your life cycle.)

Chapter one of the Department of Advanced Feng Shui discusses the gods who will descend to reside in the yearly mikeng (destiny house), who are the gods who can bring both good and bad to the fate of that year. When this is the case, worshiping to improve your luck with the gods who come down to reside in the same year of your birth is thought to be beneficial and affect you the most to rely on the gods' prestige to help protect and protect you. There is some misfortune to be alleviated as your destiny declines. At the same time, I'd like to wish you blessings to help inspire the smooth running of your business as you seek to bring prosperity and prosperity to yourself and your family.

Ji is the zodiac sign of those born in the year of the Snake or Mi Keng (House of Destiny). This year's overall picture is quite positive. Because fortunate stars are orbiting to help It will result in you being fortunate at the beginning and end of the year. However, there is a point at which you will lose money. You will be invited to join the business when there is a lot of work and money. The trade business has the potential to grow and prosper. However, be wary of slanderers because it is influenced by many unlucky stars orbiting to hurt destiny. Expected big things will fall short of the mark. The matter of fortune is still no indication of your health, and the elders in the house will become ill and should be cautious of the chaos that will visit the family. Those who are still single and in love have criteria to meet their future spouses.

Couples who have frequently quarreled with each other this year will reconcile. Please avoid overwork, inebriation, and intimacy with other girlfriends this year. You should set up sacred objects and wear amulets if you want to stop the disaster. "Manjusri Samantabhadra Buddha Ride Elephant" to request Her Majesty's assistance in promoting the work and business of destiny to prosper and progress. Wealth fortune, good health, strong health, safety, completeness, and prosperity within the family.

"Manjusri Samantabhadra Buddha Ride Elephant" as the Chinese is a Bodhisattva known for his ethics and perseverance. without fear of hardship, with a strong determination to save the world from suffering Because "elephant" is considered a tough animal, the image of Her Majesty the King's statue "Elephant Chattan white 6 tusks" is a metaphor. Saving all of the world's creatures from all suffering is a task that requires patience. and a great sacrifice to overcome all beings' passions. In general, "Bodhisattva" will be seated on the right side of the temple. Waiting to serve Buddha Shakyamuni, with "Bodhisattva Bunju the Lion" on the left. Those who worship the Bodhisattva Phu Ying frequently request his power and prestige to achieve success in various fields, such as work or business. and frequently obtains what they desire The Bodhisattva Phu Ying appeared, His left hand holding a Yuyue Jade Staff, to bestow power, dignity, and supporters to the destiny To bring you and your family only happiness, good fortune, and peace.

Those born in the year of the Snake should also wear an auspicious pendant. The "Manjusri Samantabhadra Buddha Ride Elephant" can be worn around the neck or carried with you when traveling both near and far. so that your destiny is blessed with abundant wealth Both business and trade are prospering and advancing. A happy family all year results in greater efficiency and productivity, faster than ever before.

Good Direction: Southeast, Southwest, and West
Bad Direction: Northwest
Lucky Colors: Red, Pink, Orange, and Green.
Lucky Times: 09.00 – 10.59, 15.00 – 16.59, 17.00 – 18.59.
Bad Times: 03.00 – 04.59, 21.00 – 22.59.

Good Luck For 2023